SEVEN BASICS OF BELONGING

THE MEANING OF CHURCH MEMBERSHIP

Sam Rainer

Seven Basics of Belonging: The Meaning of Church Membership

© 2021 Sam Rainer
© 2021 Church Answers

All rights reserved.
ISBN 978-0-578-85343-7

Church Answers
Franklin, TN

Printed in the United States of America

Scripture quotations are taken from the Holy Bible, New Living Translation, copyright ©1996, 2004, 2015 by Tyndale House Foundation. Used by permission of Tyndale House Publishers, Carol Stream, Illinois 60188. All rights reserved.

This book is dedicated to the Church Answers team. God's kingdom is better served because of the resources they help create for the church and her leaders.

CONTENTS

Introduction: Why Join a Church? 7
Chapter One: Saying "Yes" to God 15
Chapter Two: Making Disciples Who Make Disciples 25
Chapter Three: Reaching Outward Beyond Yourself 35
Chapter Four: Honoring God with Your Offering 45
Chapter Five: Prioritizing God's Will Through Prayer 55
Chapter Six: Keeping The Main Thing the Main Thing 65
Chapter Seven: Putting Others Before Yourself 75
Conclusion: I Joined a Church. Now What? 83
Appendix: Study Guide For Membership Class 91

INTRODUCTION
WHY JOIN A CHURCH?

You belong here! You are not here by accident. God has a plan for you, and that plan includes being a faithful and active part of a local church. Many of you are likely reading this book in connection to a new members class. You are in the right place at the right time. God wants you to be part of a church. Some of you may be reading this book out of curiosity. Perhaps you are considering joining a local church or attending for the first time in a while. I hope this brief book will prompt you to find a church where you can connect with other like-minded believers.

There are many kinds of churches. God loves them all—big, small, new, or established. Every follower of Christ is designed to be part of a local church. You are important to God. He loves you unconditionally, but He also has expectations of you through the church. In the following chapters, I will detail seven basics of belonging to a church family. First, it is critical to understand why membership matters in the first place.

Throughout the Bible, there is a clearly defined community of God. The New Testament refers to this group of people as the church. In Paul's letter to the church at Rome, he made the analogy of the church being the body of Christ. Followers of Christ are members of this body: "Just as our bodies have many parts and each part has a special function, so it is with Christ's body. We are many parts of one body, and we all belong to each other." The church universal includes every believer of all time. Christ unites all of us. But we all also have a responsibility to a local church. In Paul's letter to the church at Corinth, he writes, "All of you together are Christ's body, and each of you is a part of it."

Church membership is nothing like a country club, where you pay your dues and receive a service. Church membership is a commitment to be part of God's community through the body of Christ. In order to be part (a member) of the body (the church), you must commit to a local church. The term "local" refers to a specific location with a specific people. The term "body" represents how there are no lone ranger Christians. Those who have faith in Christ are meant to be connected to a larger group of believers through the church.

Your Commitment Matters to God

Jerry is recently married, almost a year. He is 27 years old. His wife wanted to start attending church together as they begin a family.

"I told her I was fine with whatever religion, so long as we stuck to it. She grew up in a smaller community church. The only time I attended church was holidays, and she had not been for several years."

They chose a church close to their neighborhood, and the seemingly random decision changed their lives. While both had a respect for the Bible and church, neither had heard the gospel.

"We gave our lives to Christ after attending for a couple months. Then the pastor said we needed to take a class to become official members of the church. He said something I'll never forget. The difference between attending a church and joining a church is commitment."

Jerry understood the connection between Jesus and the church.

"I now understand Jesus alone saves, but He also does not want any of His followers to be alone. Those who accept Jesus must connect to a church."

What is the big deal about membership? I recognize some of you may have experienced pain through churches that hold to an unbiblical view of membership. Unfortunately, some churches can be overbearing and harsh. Perhaps you were raised in a church that had a loose view of membership, or none at all, and now this whole idea sounds strange.

Christ committed to the church. We should commit to Him. Jesus is the Groom. We are the bride. When Paul wrote his letters, most were to the local church. The New Testament does not teach "just me, Jesus, and no one else" but rather a connection to a local church.

Our culture can push against commitment. It's too easy to "like/unlike" and "follow/unfollow." The church is your opportunity to be counter-cultural in the way Christ calls us. Practically, it's good to know who is claiming your church. Church leaders need to know who to hold accountable. In the same way schools maintain a student body, so too the church should maintain the body of Christ. Personally, committing to church membership will help you grow spiritually. God did not design us to grow in isolation. Being on a spiritual island is lonely. The church is a community of imperfect people serving a perfect Savior together. We commit together to follow Him.

Welcome to Your Church

What seemed to be random at first to Jerry became an exercise in God's sovereignty.

"We chose this church simply because it's the closest to our home, but my wife and I quickly realized God chose it for us."

God has you here for a reason. People choose churches for any number of reasons. Proximity, doctrine, personal connections, or vision are all reasons why people gravitate towards a local church. Whatever reason drew you towards your church, it is now on you to make a commitment. When you join a civic organization, there are certain expectations. The church is no different!

You need your church, and your church needs you. In the book of Philippians, Paul highlights the concept of giving and receiving. Paul gave them support through the gospel while the church supported his work. We are called to minister to others, but there will be times when we need others to minister to us. This sense of community only comes through the local church. In Christ, you don't belong everywhere and anywhere. You belong here.

Additionally, God has a mission for you. God has a plan to seek and to save the lost. He wants you to be a part of it. The church is not a destination point for crowds. The church is a vehicle designed by God to reach neighborhoods and nations. Welcome to your church. God is here. You belong here.

Introducing the Seven Basics of Belonging

In the next several chapters, I will cover the seven basics of belonging to a church. There is much more to the church than these seven basics. This book is merely an introduction to the idea of church membership.

Like the story of Jerry in this chapter, the following chapters will contain the stories of other church members. Likely, you have a different story, but I hope you can relate to some of the examples. The seven basics of belonging represent the foundation of church membership. Your church will have different doctrines, programs, schedules, and leadership than other churches. But I believe every member should fulfill these seven basics of belonging in their local church.

1. Worship: Saying "yes" to God
2. Grow: Making disciples who make disciples
3. Serve: Reaching outward beyond yourself
4. Give: Honoring God with your offering
5. Pray: Prioritizing God's will through prayer
6. Seek unity: Keeping the main thing the main thing
7. Sacrifice: Putting others before yourself

As you become more involved as a member, you will find a lot to like about your church. You will also find things you dislike. The church is like a family—some are healthier than others. The goal is to be part of the solution, not part of the problem. God placed you in this congregation for your own good. But God also placed you here for the good of others. Those inside the church and those outside the church need your help.

As we finished our conversation, Jerry noted, "Right after the pastor asked us to attend the new members class, my wife and I wondered why we would join a church. We discussed it on the way home. All of the reasons we discussed were well-intentioned but not exactly right."

Jerry paused for a moment, "The real reason you join a church is simple. Jesus is here."

Discussion Questions

1. What first drew you to this church?
2. What is your understanding of church and your role in the church?
3. How is God working in your life right now?
4. Why is commitment important for church membership?

CHAPTER ONE
SAYING "YES" TO GOD

Several years ago, I asked my worship pastor to give me the best definition of worship. His response was quick and resolute: "Saying *yes* to God."

I have never forgotten those four words. Worship is the first basic of belonging. We begin here for a reason. Worship is more than what you experience in a church service. Worship is a posture of submitting to God's will. Paul writes in Romans 12:1 to be "a living and holy sacrifice...is truly the way to worship him." What makes you a worshiper of Christ is not how in tune you sing or how much theology you know. What makes you a worshiper of Christ is if you are willing to give Him all of who you are.

The point of worship is not to get something from God but rather to get God Himself. A worshiping church desires God, not something from

God. The manner of your worship is selflessness. The motivation for your worship is the goodness and glory of God. Unfortunately, our own preferences can get in the way.

I've made lots of mistakes as a pastor. One of the more memorable instances involved a complaint about worship. My wife had led the worship service on a Sunday many years ago, and someone did not like her song selection. The upset member made her grievance loudly in the foyer so all could hear after the service.

"That wasn't real worship! How terrible!" She then added a few other choice comments about my wife.

I responded, "There are plenty of other dead churches in this town who would welcome another corpse if you don't like it here."

She never returned, which was probably for the best. But I did not help her spiritually. My unpastoral response pushed her further away from being a true worshiper. She was selfish, and I was callous. Two negatives did not make a positive.

The Problem of Personal Preferences in Worship

Everyone has personal preferences for worship. There is nothing wrong with having a favorite song or a style of music you like best. Many people attach music to key moments in their lives. Music is a powerful art form that evokes emotions. It is not a surprise that someone would be passionate for a particular song or a certain style of music! You have emotions because God has emotions, and you are made in His image. Jesus wept when He learned of the passing of His friend Lazarus. God the Father was pleased with His creation in Genesis. And we can grieve the Holy Spirit with our sin.

The emotions driving your personal preferences are not the problem. The real problem occurs when you selfishly want to impose your preferences on everyone else. A worship service does not exist for you to hear your favorite songs or your favorite style of music. I hope you have not chosen your church because of the music. I hope you chose your church because you want to give God glory with other genuine worshipers.

The Problem of Routine in Worship

Misdirected passion is a common problem in worship. I have been guilty of believing worship was "good" because one of my favorite songs was played. But there is another, more subtle problem with the way we can worship: routine.

Have you ever driven down the road, zoned out, and arrived at a place by sheer routine, only to realize that was not the place you intended to go? Habit got you there. Routine makes you numb to the obvious. I have driven to my church on several occasions while intending to go to another destination.

How do we avoid going through the motions with worship? Sunday mornings can become routine, even for faithful people who have a deep love for Jesus and His church. What is good worship? And what is bad worship?

Pursuing Good Worship and Avoiding Bad Worship

Bad worship is using anything other than Jesus to get closer to God. In fact, good things can become bad things when you make them God things. When you worship your marriage, your children, a sports team, or anything other than Jesus, that thing—even if it is good—will sour because you are placing it in front of God. Is something or someone in front of Jesus in your life? Does something or someone have a higher priority? When you make worship a priority of church membership, then you consistently work to align yourself with God's will. You say "yes" to God.

Good worship is an awareness you are in the presence of God. Worship is not that which is most inspirational, most beautiful, most historical, most cherished, most trendy, or most popular. Worship is an awareness by Christ's body that the people are together with the Spirit of God.

When the church has good worship, two important results occur. First, an internal unity occurs within the body. The people are unified as one voice together. Generations unite regardless of style. Song selection no longer matters. Your concern is for the spiritual development of others. Second, good worship becomes attractive to those outside the church. You care more about what will draw in those who do not believe in Jesus, and you care less about what pleases you. True worshipers become backyard missionaries. What you experience in a church service compels you to share Christ with the people in proximity to you.

Healthy Worship Is Regular Worship

Good worship is never occasional. God expects you to worship Him regularly! I once joked in a new membership class that God does not want CEO worship. Unfortunately, I did not explain the acronym thinking that everyone knew it meant "Christmas and Easter only." After the class, a man came up to me and wanted to know why CEO worship was a problem.

"I didn't want to say anything in front of everyone, but I'm the chief executive officer at my company."

Thankfully, he laughed when I explained the joke.

Worship attendance is like exercise. When you go twice a year, it hurts. A regular exercise program builds your strength and health, but it takes time. You do not get much healthier when you work out sporadically and without much discipline. The same principle applies to your worship.

Ask someone with a regular exercise routine about a workout on Tuesday four months ago. Unless something extraordinary happened, I doubt this person could give you details. The same is true of your worship. You will not remember every worship experience, every point of every sermon, or every lesson at church. But like exercise, the cumulative effect of regular worship makes you stronger and healthier. One of the best ways to stay healthy spiritually is to attend weekly worship services at your church. The more regular you are in worship, the more you will say "yes" to God.

True worship is always focused on God. You should not get too caught up in the look of the worship space, the style of the music, or what others think. Worship is an all-encompassing submission to Jesus. A worshiping church will pray, elevate the study of God's Word, sing together, participate in communion, and serve others. Your worship is not limited to a single experience of one aspect of what happens when the church gathers. The best worship occurs when you surrender to God's will.

How do we get to the point where it's not about us? Where our worship is not about getting from God but rather getting God? It's possible through the cross of Christ. The gospel helps us see God not as *useful* but as *worthy*. God does a lot of things, but we don't worship Him because He's useful to us. We worship because only He is worthy. That's our worship with God. We don't give ourselves to get from God. We give ourselves to get God Himself. This first basic of belonging begins with a simple premise. Are you willing to say "yes" to God? Are you willing to worship Him for who He is and not just what He provides? If so, then you're ready for our next basic of belonging to the church: grow.

Discussion Questions

1. How can we make worship all about God and not about us?
2. What can you do to prepare your heart for a worship service?
3. How do we get distracted in our worship?
4. Why should a church expect members to worship?

CHAPTER TWO
MAKING DISCIPLES WHO MAKE DISCIPLES

A Christian is someone who belongs to Christ. A disciple is someone who follows Christ. You can't claim to belong to Christ if you are not willing to follow Him. Becoming a Christian is something that happens at a specific point in time. Many of you may have written the date of your salvation in your Bibles. I don't remember the exact date, but I have a memory of the moment. I was 7 years old, and I accepted Christ in a church service when my dad was preaching. It was a sunny winter morning, and sunbeams were shining through the stained-glass windows.

Some of you may not remember exactly when you were saved by Jesus, but you have an assurance of His salvation. At a point in your past, God sovereignly saved you. It's at this point when you should start following Christ. Since you belong to

Him, you follow Him. Your lifelong journey—with all the ups and downs—is discipleship. The purpose of following Jesus is to be more like Him. In fact, discipleship in its simplest form is defined as being more like Christ.

In the Gospels, Jesus uses the term *disciples* to describe those who completely devoted themselves to Him. The book of Acts records that these followers of Christ were called "Christians." You may use some different terms to describe your relationship with Jesus. There are certainly many other ways to define how you follow Christ. This process fills volumes of books, and some of the most known and well-loved Christian classics are about discipleship. I could never match these works in this chapter, but I hope to inspire you to dig deeper through your church.

Whatever term you use, the Bible is clear. You are to grow spiritually, and you are to help others grow as well. The reason "grow" is our second basic of belonging is because the New Testament is clear that spiritual growth is a key purpose of the church. This purpose has two basic aims: A deeper faith individually and a wider reach corporately. You grow deeper individually by becoming more mature in the Christian faith. The church is mandated to grow wider numerically by multiplying believers by reaching others for Christ. All churches and all Christians are called to make disciples who make disciples.

You Do Not Grow Alone

You need the church to grow spiritually because you can't grow alone. A key part of having a relationship with someone is presence. Just being there is important. We say things like, "I'm here for you. I'm around. I'm available. I can be there." These phrases are deeper than mere platitudes. They represent the ministry of presence. Some people are extroverts, and others are introverts. Some like the crowd while others prefer a smaller group. Whatever your personality, you need people.

My wife's love language is quality time. By quality, it means we could be doing just about anything so long as it's done together. Whether I surprise her with an extravagant vacation or pull out a board game, she is happy to be with her family.

Sometimes all you need to know is that you

are not alone. God created us as social creatures because He is social. There is a perfect and beautiful relationship within the Trinity—the Father with the Son with the Spirit. This relationship can be perplexing and mysterious, but it is also reassuring. God wants to be with us. We should want to be with Him. God also wants us to be with each other. Spiritually, you do not grow by yourself. Nobody can grow alone. Spiritual growth occurs in proximity to others. Isolation does not produce disciples. Disciples are made through the ministry of the church.

The Five Times Factor of a Small Group

You are five times more likely to stay in a church if you join a group. Here are the facts. Eighty-three percent of people will stay in a church if they attend worship services and also join a group. However, only 16 percent of people will stay in the church if they attend a worship service only and never join a group. Most people *start* attending a church through the worship service, but most people *stay* in a church because of their connection to a group.

These groups have many different names and many different forms, but they main thing is that you are in one regularly. Some churches have Sunday school, community groups, family groups, Bible studies, or life groups. Some groups are ongoing, while others have a set number of weeks. Some groups go deep into Scripture. Others include introductory Bible lessons. Some groups are led by master teachers. Others are more about conversations or community. Some groups are age-segmented, while others are created by common interests. Whatever you call your group and whatever your group looks like, it is one of the most important ways in which you will grow spiritually and one of the most important ways you will invest in others.

We have some groups at my church that have been meeting together for decades. They are family. The people in these groups have grown up together, raised families together, and supported each other through the highs and lows of life. A few years ago, we did some research on why young people drop out of the church. One of the biggest reasons is they lack a connection to more mature disciples. We found a positive correlation: The more adults that invest in the life of a young person, the more likely that young person will stay in the church. Most people do not just decide one day to leave the church. They fade and slowly start attending less. The way to stop the fade is building a connection to a small group.

Hebrews 10:24-25 informs us that the reason we gather as a church is to encourage and motivate each other to acts of love and good works. Maybe you've had a bad church experience. Maybe you're thinking, "A relationship with Jesus is *personal*, not *institutional*. Why do I really need a group in the church?" If you have a similar thought, then I sympathize. The church is more of an organism than it is an organization. God makes the church alive! To thrive, the members of the church must be together and get involved in each other's lives. Every church structures groups in a different way. The main thing you can do is commit to be involved in one. Do you want to grow spiritually? Get involved in a group at your church.

The Discipline and Accountability of Spiritual Growth

Some people are more disciplined than others, but even extreme self-starters need accountability. You need people around you asking, "How can I help you grow?" Being a disciple of Jesus requires intentionality, thoughtfulness, and faithfulness. You need the support and encouragement of a local church to grow.

Spiritual growth occurs in many ways. You grow through the spiritual disciplines like fasting, prayer, confession, and meditation. Daily Bible reading and personal devotional time are imperative to being a follower of Christ. You must listen to sermons regularly and learn from skilled and mature teachers and preachers. And, as I have mentioned, you must be active in a group setting with other like-minded believers.

You are more likely to stick to a plan of spiritual growth with the support of other people. Maintaining the discipline to grow means asking other people to hold you accountable, especially in areas where you struggle. You cannot grow alone. Complete isolation is not God's design.

We are made in God's image. As social beings,

we reflect the social nature of the Trinity. God is three Persons: Father, Son, and Holy Spirit. He is relational, and we need godly relationships with other people.

Get involved in a group. Be part of the movement to make disciples who make disciples. You need your church. And your church needs you.

Discussion Questions

1. How do you define spiritual maturity?
2. Who has invested in you spiritually? How did this person help you grow?
3. Why is it important you grow with others and not alone?
4. What is your favorite Bible study or Bible passage? Why is it your favorite?

CHAPTER THREE
REACHING OUTWARD BEYOND YOURSELF

Churches are not islands in the community, set up to isolate believers from the ails of society. The walls of the church are not protective barriers to community problems. Quite the opposite—the church should be the vehicle by which people are sent into the hardest, darkest parts of the neighborhood.

You can serve in many ways. There is service within the church. Perhaps you are gifted with hospitality and have a desire to make your church a welcoming environment for guests. Hospitality is one of the most underrated and underutilized gifts in the church today. There is also service that extends beyond the church body. My church, for example, has a large number of foster families.

Our county is first in removal rates of children in all of Florida. Of the five hundred children removed from their homes last year, over half of them are directly attributed to substance abuse. Most of the children removed are under the age of 5.

Whatever issues are producing foster children are often the core of a community's sins. Take a foster child into your home, and you are immediately connected to some of the most difficult issues in your community. In our case, it's opioid addiction. Our children's ministry is full of foster kids. Here is what I love about how my church is ministering to these children: The name tags of our foster children don't have a special label designated them as being fostered. These children are part of our homes, which means they are part of our church family. We've opened our doors to the worst problem in our community, and God brought us beautiful children who need to hear good news.

Jesus makes a clear statement in Mark's gospel: "For even the Son of Man came not to be served but to serve others and to give his life as a ransom for many." The King of kings serves. If God Himself expects to serve, then you should as well. The call of every Christian is to be selfless (others first), not selfish (ourselves first).

Our third basic of belonging is serving: reaching outward beyond yourself. It's not about you! It's about sharing with others, reaching others, and serving others. The way the church fulfills God's outward calling is through serving.

Greatness in God's Kingdom

In 100 years, assuming Christ does not return, the goal of your church is to be doing God's work in your current location. Your service today is the foundation for the next 100 years of work. The churches that stand the test of time are filled with servant leaders, people who put others before themselves. An enduring church serves like Jesus.

In Mark 10, James and John believe they are worthy of the highest place of honor in God's kingdom. They believe they are worthy of this prominence.

Jesus asks them, "Are you able to endure suffering like Me?"

James and John reply, "Yes, we are!"

Jesus tells them, "You don't know what you are asking."

Greatness in God's kingdom comes through serving. How did Jesus serve? He gave His life! We've got to be willing to lay it all out there so others can hear the good news. God's kingdom is eternal because of the sacrifice of Christ. Your church will endure because the people give of themselves to God's mission. To be *saved* by Jesus is to be *sent* by Jesus. And the way you can live sent is to serve through the bride of Christ, His church.

Ian and Christine are two of my favorite servants of Christ. They are married, and both are retired police officers. Their calling to serve is simple—take care of the homeless in their community every day of the year. They wash the feet of the people they once arrested. They rarely take breaks or vacations. When you mingle with 200 homeless people every day, it gets a little messy. The mess does not bother Ian and Christine. You can grow slowly in wisdom and maturity by sitting in pews, but you make leaps when you minister on the streets. Greatness is found among the least of these in your community. You may not have a large homeless population around your church, but every place has a group of people who need help. When you serve them, you find God's greatness.

Five Steps to Serving through Your Church

According to 2 Corinthians 5:14, the motivating factor for serving is Christ's love. If you love Jesus, then you will be compelled to serve others through His church. I understand you may be new to church and serving is a new concept. Or perhaps you were raised in the church but never considered serving because it was not emphasized. Belonging to a church means serving through the church. These next five steps will help you get started.

Step one: Look for opportunities. Start observing what your church is doing. Ask other members where they serve and shadow them in their ministry areas. The more you are aware, the more quickly you will find your fit and the better you can help others find their fit. You may not find your place to serve right away, but you can go ahead and start reserving time on your calendar as you observe.

Step two: Volunteer where there is a need.

Perhaps your calling isn't to find the perfect fit for you but rather to fill in the gaps where the church is short volunteers. Invest yourself where the fruit of ministry is occurring. Listen to your leaders and what they say are the areas where more help is required. When you have a posture of service, it is not so much about what you want to do and rather about what needs to be done.

Step three: Take the initiative! You should not wait for someone to "volun-told" you. Church leaders often must scramble for volunteers and end up twisting arms to fill necessary spots. Start your church membership by telling the leadership you are ready to begin right away. I don't believe I've ever met a church member that said he or she regretted taking the initiative to serve.

Step four: Invite your neighbors to church. Serving always compels you outward. One of the best ways to serve Jesus is to invite others to be part of His body. Are people receptive to coming to church? Yes! In fact, 80 percent of people are receptive to coming to church *if invited*. Of course, not everyone will come each time you invite them, but they are willing to listen to you. Inviting people to church is one of the best ways to move outward as a follower of Christ.

Step five: Share Jesus with people. Inviting people to church is critically important, but it is not evangelism. If you know Jesus, then you have the best news anyone can hear. People need to hear the gospel from you! Sharing how Jesus saves is the reason why you serve. Of course, every church should want to help people who have physical needs. But the reason we serve others is to share how they can be saved eternally.

In the New Testament, there is a transition between the four Gospels and the book of Acts. In the Gospels, Jesus is present on this earth. At the beginning of Acts, Jesus ascends into heaven. When He returns to His throne in heaven, Jesus tells His followers about the mission of the church. Where Christ's work on earth ends, our work as the church begins. The Gospels record Jesus movement *towards* Jerusalem. The book of Acts records the church's movement *outward* from Jerusalem. Jesus was determined to fulfill God's plan of saving the world through His sacrifice on the cross. We should be determined to fulfill God's mission of getting the good news of Jesus to the ends of the earth.

We are the rest of the story. We are the ones completing what began in Acts. As you serve in your church, you are doing kingdom work for Jesus. It's not really about you, or even your church. It's about Christ Himself.

Discussion Questions

1. What are some ways you can use your gifts to serve others?
2. How is Jesus the example for serving in the church?
3. Describe someone you know who acts selflessly. How do they serve others?
4. Who can you invite to church? How will you invite them?

CHAPTER FOUR
HONORING GOD WITH YOUR OFFERING

One of my pet peeves is when my wife or one of my daughters asks for a bite of what is on my plate. When I fill my plate, I get exactly what I want—no less and no more. Then one of them comes along and says, "That looks good. Can I have a bite?"

My response is always the same: "No."

Then an argument ensues.

"Why don't you get your own? You can have a whole piece to yourself."

"But I don't want a whole piece. I just want a bite."

The whole exchange is annoying, but we do the same thing with God. We have our stuff, our things, and our money. It's all ours, or so we like to think. Then we feel as if God is pestering us for a bite when He asks us to give our offerings.

Our fourth basic of belonging is giving. Up to

this point, the expectations of church membership have not been controversial. I believe most who join a church expect to attend worship frequently, be involved in a group or Bible study, and serve in the church. This expectation has the potential to be tense. But it doesn't have to be.

Psalm 107 begins with the imperative of giving: "Give thanks to the Lord, for he is good!" What do we give to God? Thanks! Why do we give thanks to God? It's because God is faithful and loving. A faithful church is a giving church, and a faithful believer is constantly giving thanks to God.

The one thing most Christians can agree on is the loving nature of God. Indeed, 1 John 4:8 tells us, "God is love." The issue is we don't get to define God's love any way we choose. We dishonor Him when we redefine His terms of love. One way we embrace God's love is through the act of giving, which is one of the main ways we worship Him.

A pastor friend of mine says it well: "Most people tip 10 to 15 percent even for bad service. For Christians who struggle giving, has God's service to you been that bad?" My goal in this chapter is not to guilt you into giving to God. Rather, I want God to love you into giving to Him. Guilt is a terrible motivator with a short duration. Just about any pastor can increase the offering by putting parishioners through a guilt trip about giving, but it lasts only about one or two weeks. The better motivator for giving is God's love.

Every Gift Matters to God

Luke records the story of a giving widow. Jesus was observing people dropping their gifts in the collection box at the temple. The rich were bringing their gifts. Then a poor widow was only able to give two small coins. Jesus uses her example as a teaching moment. He points out how she gave everything she had while others only gave from surplus.

I realize many of you are not wealthy. Some of you may be living in poverty. For those who struggle financially, Jesus teaches there is incredible spiritual power in the small gifts from people who have nothing from which to give.

God may bless (or not bless) your church depending on how you give. I am convinced some churches do not experience revival because the people are holding back their giving from God.

For those of you who are financially secure, do not fear giving like the rich, young ruler. In Luke 18, Jesus interacts with this man who believes he has done enough to gain eternal life. Jesus reminds him that eternity is not based upon a sliding scale of good works. Rather, eternity is given to those who surrender all to Jesus. In one of the hardest verses in the Bible, the rich man refuses God's grace because he could not give up his possessions. Luke records the man "became very sad, for he was very rich."

What is your goal with "your" money? Is it a higher standard of living? Or is it a higher standard of giving? Jesus teaches that both the rich and the poor can live a righteous life as long as we make generosity our goal. Jesus is King over everything. He owns it all. But when Christ came to earth, He was poor. He had no place to lay His head and owned only one pair of sandals.

The issue is *not* wealth—whether you've got it or not. The issue is whether you are pursuing God or forgetting God. Every one of your giving contributions matter to God. Every gift is important to God. But our calling is not to give from a place of surplus. Our calling is to give from a place of sacrifice.

Erik and Emily are in their early 40s and have been tithing as a couple since their marriage began 20 years ago.

"We were convicted that God calls us to give 10 percent of our income, and it was hard when we made so little in our 20s."

Over time, both received several promotions. As their income went up, they continued to tithe.

"At the beginning of our marriage, I believe our combined income was not even $30,000 annually. It was hard to give 10 percent in those early years. Frankly, giving 10 percent got easier as we started making more. We did not live above our means and saved regularly. We were disciplined with our money."

They recently bought their dream home—a fixer-upper in the perfect neighborhood. Then God hit them with an unexpected conviction.

"God told us to give above the tithe. The Holy Spirit led us to give above our normal amount whatever we were going to spend fixing up our home."

To accomplish this goal, they had to sacrifice the way they lived. They still renovated their home, but they gave up other items. Erik sold his antique car. Emily sold jewelry. They cut their vacation budget and sent their oldest daughter to a state university instead of a private college. By most standards, they are still doing well. But they changed the way they lived to give what God had called them to give. This level of giving is sacrificial.

Sacrificial Giving Changes You

Sacrificial giving is the antidote to greed. There are two types of greed. The first is driven by the desire for more stuff. The second is driven by the desire for more security. Those who succumb to greed often want more material goods or more wealth. When you want *more*, you will give *less*. But another form of greed is driven by a desire to be safe. Some people do not collect material goods or wealth, but large amounts of cash in their bank accounts make them feel in control and safe.

Greed and materialism blind you. They distort the way you see the world. Materialists don't know they have materialism. I've never done a counseling session on materialism or greed. Pride, lust, bitterness...yes, but never greed.

Greed is a blinding sin. With adultery, you know what you've done. No one accidentally steals.

Whether you want more stuff or more security, 1 Timothy 6:10 says, "For the love of money is the root of all kinds of evil. And some people, craving money, have wandered from the true faith and pierced themselves with many sorrows." You can love money and crave money because you want more stuff or because you want to be more security. Both forms of greed are dangerous to your spiritual development.

How is sacrificial giving the solution to the problem of greed? When you give sacrificially, it changes you spiritually! In fact, if what you are giving does not cause you to change your lifestyle, then it is not sacrificial. Not all giving is sacrificial, and that's not necessarily a bad thing. When you leave a great tip, the extra $20 is generous, but it doesn't hurt to give it. When you buy a hungry person a meal, it's generous, but it doesn't hurt to give the meal. You may give $5, $10, $50, or more to any number of causes—all of which are generous. Generosity becomes sacrificial when it starts to hurt.

Sacrificial giving changes your lifestyle. In

order to give sacrificially, you must change the way you live. The church needs people to be generous. It's how ministry happens and how the lights in the building stay on. But God calls all believers to change the way they live to give to Him as an act of worship. This is the calling of the widow's two small coins. The best way to unwind greed in your life is to give sacrificially. They best way to prevent greed is to give sacrificially.

Why should we be a sacrificial part of the body of Christ? Sacrificial giving is how the church unites for the cause of Christ. This level of giving brings you closer to God and is a true investment in eternity. Ultimately, God does not need your money. He created the world; He owns it all. What God desires is all your heart, soul, and mind. The only way you can give Him all of who you are is through sacrifice.

Discussion Questions

1. Why does every gift, whether large or small, matter to God?
2. Describe your views of generosity. Why does God call us to be generous?
3. How does living sacrificially impact your giving?
4. What might regular giving do for our attitudes?

CHAPTER FIVE
PRIORITIZING GOD'S WILL THROUGH PRAYER

Prayer is a challenging spiritual discipline. The concept is not hard to understand. You communicate with God and listen to Him. Prayer is difficult not in concept but in practice. There is no instant gratification with prayer. You do not have a message read feature or push notification for prayer like you do with phones.

Is prayer really that important? In my experience as a pastor, church members pray, but it is more during times of convenience or crisis. Prayer happens when people have the time or when their world starts to crumble. Making prayer a spiritual discipline is not common enough among church members. Our fifth basic of belonging is often overlooked as an expectation of church membership, but it is critical to your spiritual health. Prayer is the way you demonstrate faith in God's

Word and trust in His will. You cannot prioritize God's will without praying!

What Prayer is All About

Margaret and Pat approached me with a request: "We think our church should pray more."

"It's hard to disagree with that."

They had an idea about an addition to our prayer ministry. They would gather a group of their friends and pray specifically for our missionaries, friends and family who need to know Christ, and needs in the neighborhood. They had recognized something that is prevalent in many churches.

"Most of our request are about physical needs. We enjoy praying for them, but we also believe God wants us to direct our prayers beyond the medical problems of members in the church."

As you can imagine, these two women are among the biggest blessings in my church. Their prayers help prioritize God's will for our entire church. Though many members may not know this prayer group, the direction of our church depends on them. We are a better church because they pray to seek God's will rather than bringing God a laundry list of requests.

In Luke 11:1, the disciples ask Jesus, "Lord, teach us to pray." Jesus then uses the Lord's Prayer as a teaching tool. When you examine the Lord's Prayer, you will notice it starts with God, not us. The famous prayer begins with an acknowledgement of who God is—our Father. This pattern is found throughout the Bible. The creation account in Genesis 1 starts with God: "In the beginning God..." The ubiquitous John 3:16 begins with God loving the world. The same principle applies to the Lord's Prayer. Prayer is all about God in the same way everything else should be all about God. As Jesus states in Matthew 6, prayer is about His name, His kingdom, and His will.

Prayer is not about prayer. A cell phone does not exist for itself. It is a tool for connectivity. Prayer is a way we relate to God. When you pray, you give God glory. Every prayer is an opportunity to witness the glory of God! Prayer helps us connect two concepts. First, God is infinite, awesome, and beyond us. Second, God is near to us—right here, right now. Prayer is the way finite people communicate with an infinite God.

The Bible is *not* about us. The Bible is about God first. Proper prayer puts God first. Prayer is not about trying to get God to do our will on earth but rather us attempting to do God's will on earth. Prayer is all about God, not us.

The Benefits of an Ongoing Conversation with God

Prayer is not about you, but the good news is God does care about you. When you place your faith in God through prayer, He provides His will to you. In 1 Thessalonians 5, Paul gives some final advice to a church he loves. In this advice, a helpful list emerges.

"Always be joyful. Never stop praying. Be thankful in all circumstances, for this is God's will for you who belong to Christ Jesus."

Notice the pattern here. In order to pursue what is good (God's will), we have to pray constantly and rejoice always. The path to joy is God's will, and the only way to find this path is through the discipline of regular prayer. When Paul writes to the Philippian church, he emphasizes the importance of prayer again.

"Pray about everything. Tell God what you

need, and thank him for all he has done."

Your life should be an ongoing conversation with God. Get into your phone and check your text messages. I imagine there are some people you text daily, if not more often. And you text people all day long. Why not talk to God in the same way?

Prayer is a strategy for life. Prayer is a way to discern the daily tactics for living that enable you to thrive spiritually. Prayer is not passive resignation. It's not a last resort!

"Nothing else worked, so I guess I'll pray" is one of the weakest ways to talk to the sovereign Creator of the universe. God is in control, so you should talk to Him in a way that recognizes His power. A powerful prayer is one that rests in God's sovereignty and trusts in His grace. This trusting and resting is the very definition of prayer. It is not our prayers that overcome. It is God who overcomes, and we pray to Him.

Prayer is important because it connects the dots of the Christian life. Your ongoing communication with God is the link between much of what we do as Christians. Prayer aids evangelism. In Luke 10, Jesus instructs His followers to pray for a harvest, then He tells them to go. In James 1, prayer is a pathway to wisdom. Both Jesus and Isaiah remind us that God's house will be one of prayer. Paul connects his partnership with the church through prayer. And Jesus Himself grew spiritually as a boy by being with His heavenly Father.

When you prioritize prayer, you are making God's will your priority. As we learn though the interaction with Jesus and His disciples in Luke 11, prayer must be taught. You can learn more about God and yourself through prayer. You can get better at prayer by practicing it. You're not always going to get prayer right in the same way your kids do not always communicate well with you. But God always wants to hear from you, and He enjoys your genuine efforts to talk with Him.

The Place and Time of Prayer

Church members should pray both privately and corporately. You need time alone with God, and you need to seek Him through the collective wisdom of others. The beauty of prayer is you can do it anywhere. Pray with others in a worship gathering and in a prayer meeting. Pray with your Bible study group. Pray every day with your spouse and your family. Lead your children by teaching them to pray. You also need to pray alone. Dedicate daily time to God, even if this time is five or ten minutes. Even the busiest people have time to pray!

God is ready to listen at any moment. He hears you at moments of unexpected crisis. God understands your situation. Sometimes all you can do is express a quick and silent prayer.

When you give a short prayer walking into what you know will be a stressful meeting, God is listening. When you offer rapid fire praises while you are driving, God is listening. God hears instantaneous prayers—every word. But you should also dedicate time to pray, and scheduling this time is necessary. You will make time for what is important to you. I enjoy watching baseball, and the games often have strange start times. For example, some games will begin at ten minutes after the top of the hour. Whatever the start time, I make sure not to miss the key games. If you get to the airport on time for a flight, if you can schedule your day around the start time of a sports game, then you can make time for prayer. Prayer is a spiritual *discipline*. Like exercise or any other priority, you have to make the time.

Pray with faith. People who do not think they will get answers to their prayers will likely not notice when God answers them! One of the more common questions Christians ask involves prayer: "Does God hear me?" He does. But there is a better question.

Do my prayers align my will with God's will?

Discussion Questions

1. Where do you like to pray?
2. How has God answered a prayer in your life?
3. Why is waiting for God's timing in our prayers so hard?
4. What are some specific items you pray for regularly?

CHAPTER SIX
KEEPING THE MAIN THING THE MAIN THING

I noticed the group of Indians in our church foyer. They seemed to be happy, but it was obvious they had no idea where they were.

"How did they get here?" I asked a greeter.

"Randall brought them."

They were engineering students at the local university. Randall had pulled up by the bus stop, and they got on the church bus thinking it would follow the usual route. Whether or not Randall intentionally made this move, he was known to bring all sorts of people to church, especially those who were not like him.

Randall was a big, burly dude who wore overalls and talked with a thick Southern accent. He had never been to India and knew nothing of their culture. That did not stop him from picking them up and bringing them to church. Randall had one mission in life: Be as kind as possible to everyone and connect as many people to Jesus as he could. He genuinely cared about people and was passionate about the gospel.

He was always drawing people around him who were not like him. When he led a single mom and her daughter to Christ, I told him, "You need to baptize them."

"No way," he replied, "I'm not worthy of doing something like that."

After I pushed him to do it, he finally agreed. He was nervous and sweaty when he entered the baptistry, but there was no mistaking the big smile on his face. Randall beamed as this mom and her daughter were baptized. He followed them out of the baptistry, made his way to the changing room, collapsed in a heap, and died immediately of a massive heart attack.

I will never forget talking with Randall's wife—now a widow—shortly afterwards. Did nerves cause the heart attack? Was I to blame for pushing him to do the baptism?

I mumbled, "I might have killed Randall."

"No," she was firm. "God foreordained that heart attack. It was going to happen no matter what."

Then we both realized Randall's last words on this earth. "In the name of the Father, the Son, and the Holy Spirit." Since he was faithful, God let Randall's last action be baptizing another believer. I believe the first words Randall heard as he approached heaven were "well done good and faithful servant."

Our sixth basic of belonging is unity. As a church member, you must keep the main thing the main thing. The goal of every church member is to share the love of Christ with a lost world.

Seeking Unity as an Act of Love

A unified church is driven by love. Unfortunately, churches can be unloving and defined by disunity. Churches can have the wrong definition of love. Churches can be unified around the wrong things. How do we know we are unified in Christ and showing love in a way that honors God?

Colossians 3:17 reminds us, "And whatever you do or say, do it as a representative of the Lord Jesus." Be what you are. The church is most unified when the members live out who they are. If you are a Christian, then you should live and love like a Christian. You are saved, so live like you are saved.

Unity and the message of the gospel are inseparable concepts. The most unified churches are the most focused on the gospel. The healthiest churches inwardly are the most focused outwardly.

Ephesians 4 brings out the concept of unity in diversity. The passage records a critical lesson: "Always be humble and gentle. Be patient with each other, making allowance for each other's faults because of your love. Make every effort to keep yourselves united in the Spirit, binding yourselves together with peace."

Unity is internal and organic, something that you seek. Uniformity is institution and forced upon you. When a private school requires all students to wear the same uniforms, this uniformity does not necessarily engender unity. The same is true of a professional sports team. The uniform is a good reminder of being on the same team, but the uniform alone cannot produce unity. I don't know of a church that has a specific dress code, nor would I recommend it. You can still be you individually, but God demands unity in the church. God's Word and God's mission should be the unifying force of every church.

Seeking unity is an act of love. I realize not everyone is easy to love. The toughest people to love are the best opportunities to love others like Jesus.

The Secret Power of the Golden Rule

You've probably heard of the Golden Rule, found in Luke 6:31, "Do to others as you would like them to do to you." This verse is located in the same section that begins, "Love your enemies." It is one thing to love people who are kind to you, but it's much harder to love those whom you consider enemies. The secret power of the Golden Rule is showing love to those who you do not believe deserve it.

Who are your enemies? Perhaps you are thinking of a foreign power, an enemy of the state. Maybe you are thinking about an oppressive tyrant or a corrupt business leader dealing in something illicit. These kinds of enemies are far away and often do not bring immediate harm into our lives. I will ask the question a different way.

Who causes you the most problems in your life? Now you are likely thinking of someone close. Jesus says love them.

My brothers and I had mortal enemies growing up. Alma and Arthur lived next door. The first time we saw them, we waved. They yelled at us to leave them alone. If we came within a couple of feet of a single blade of grass in their yard, we were told in explicit terms to stay away. I learned a lot of new and inappropriate terms from them.

Rather than doing our best to accommodate them, my brothers and I tossed dead rats over their fence and into their yard. They hated us. We returned hate to them. The mutual hatred remained until we moved.

How do we typically respond to those who hate us? We hate them back! It's a natural, and sinful, response. Jesus tells us to live in a different way. He says you should be an active agent of good for your neighbor, the cube dweller next to you, that person at school who torments you, bullies, and jerks.

In place of revenge, Jesus established the Golden Rule. Church members are to treat others the way they want to be treated. Unfortunately, we can demand our rights. We want what is ours. We want what we can rightfully claim. If you were an unbeliever looking at God's people in the church, what would you expect a Christ-follower to do? Love! This love is impossible without Jesus. To show it, we must die to ourselves and take on Christ. In this way, church members are unified in self-denial.

It's one thing to love tough neighbors who don't know Jesus. But what about the people *in* the church who are difficult? Accountability is important. Sometimes it's necessary to call out people for being divisive. Your church likely has a process for doing this. But let me offer you a challenge: Don't just *desire* unity, *seek* unity. What often gets passed off as charity really isn't. We will do good knowing we get something in return. Anyone can return love for love. Our goal is a deeper love and a stronger unity.

At the core of every healthy church is unity. And what do you find at the core? Healthy individuals who are working tirelessly to keep the main thing the main thing. You should speak up against church bullies. You will need to sacrifice your own preferences so others can know

Christ. Additionally, challenge your peers not to be selfish with their own preferences. And vocalize your encouragement of leadership. Keep the main thing the main thing.

Discussion Questions

1. Name someone who lives out the Golden Rule. How do they act?
2. Why is unity necessary for church health? How is division unhealthy?
3. What can you do personally to seek unity?
4. How can you challenge your peers in the church to unity?

CHAPTER SEVEN
PUTTING OTHERS BEFORE YOURSELF

The degree to which you are willing to sacrifice gives a window into your soul. Sacrifice demonstrates how much you are willing to attain something. We sacrifice buying something we want today to prepare for retirement tomorrow. Professional athletes sacrifice time to train, the same with master musicians. Parents sacrifice personal desires to raise children. Every decision in favor of one area is a decision to deny another area of your life.

The last basic of belonging to a church is sacrifice. Sacrifice in the church means putting God's work above your preferences and putting others before yourself.

Clem approached his pastor, "I want to cover the cost of your new air conditioning system."

The pastor was shocked. He had only briefly mentioned the unexpected expense to a couple of leaders. How did Clem find out?

"You don't need to do that. We can take the money out of savings."

"I know you are careful with your money, pastor. It does not surprise me that you have an emergency savings fund. But this is not an argument or a negotiation. God told me to pay for it."

Clem was a retired auto worker, and he did not have a large net worth. The pastor wondered where Clem would get the money. The church had a culture of generosity. Many people gave gift cards, especially during pastor appreciation month and around Easter. But Clem was making an offer that was truly sacrificial.

"I don't expect you or anyone else—"

"Pastor, it's done. You will offend me if you refuse."

Clem is an example of sacrifice, reflecting one of Christ's core attributes. When Jesus came to earth, He "gave up his divine privileges" and "took the humble position of a slave." Paul writes in his letter to the Philippian that Jesus did not cling to His equality with God and humbled Himself to a death on the cross. You are saved through this sacrifice. Through the cross, Jesus becomes our

Mediator—a bridge across the chasm of sin that separates us from the Father. Jesus was willing to sacrifice everything to accomplish God's plan of redemption.

When we accept Jesus, our calling is to mirror His sacrifice. By clinging to our preferences, our money, our schedules, and our own desires, we don't glorify God or reflect Jesus.

You do not join a church to see what you can get out of it. You join a church to give into the body of Christ. When looking for a church, the temptation is to ask the wrong questions. Does the music style fit my taste? Do they have the programs I prefer? Are the sermons the length I like? Joining a church should be an act of sacrifice, not an exercise in weighing your preferences. You join a church to sacrifice for God's mission to save the world. It's about kingdom work, not your preferences.

The Paradox of a Living Sacrifice

Tina saw the pastor scrambling and knew exactly what was happening. The student band was leading worship, and the sound was obviously too loud.

"Stop worrying about the sound. I've got it

covered." She yelled in his ear above the deafening roar of guitars and drums.

The pastor calmed down and sat with his family. His daughter was playing bass, and she saw him run to the sound booth.

Now that Tina was handling the situation, there would be no blowback. She was the matriarch of the church, and nobody argued with her. Everyone respected her. When Tina turned 80 years old, she decided to fight for the future of the church and root out the culture of personal preferences. That was six years ago.

At first, some of her peers thought something was wrong. Tina had a fiery reputation and even helped push out a pastor two decades prior. Something clicked on her 80th birthday.

"I realized I was wrong. My preferences would not last beyond me, and it's completely selfish to impose them on others. Why would I ask the teenagers to suffer through my preferences until I die? My generation needs to give up our desires so the younger generation can grow in Christ."

What is even more amazing is Tina's entire family returned to the church once she changed her attitude. Four generations now worshiped together.

Tina is an example of a living sacrifice. The term is intentionally a paradox. How can you be a living sacrifice? In the Old Testament, sacrifice implies killing and death. The New Testament brings this concept more to light. In fact, Romans 12:1 offers an explanation.

"And so, dear brothers and sisters, I plead with you to give your bodies to God because of all he has done for you. Let them be a living and holy sacrifice—the kind he will find acceptable. This is truly the way to worship him."

To be a living sacrifice is to die to yourself over and over and over. You put to death the idea that your life is your own, that you have the right to live as you choose. Notice the nouns in the above verse. Brothers, sisters, and bodies are all plural, which makes sense. The church is multiple people, not just one person. But there is another noun that is singular: sacrifice. The verse does not say multiple people in the church make many different sacrifices. What it does say is multiple people in the church make one sacrifice.

The missing "s" is intentional. It's not *sacrifices*, plural. It's *sacrifice*, singular. As the church, we don't make individual sacrifices. We unite and make one sacrifice together. Your church needs you. Your church expects you to accomplish God's calling on your life. God wants you to thrive spiritually at your church. But none of this can happen without sacrifice. In many ways all the other expectations lead up to this one. Sacrifice is the result of all the other basics of belonging.

You worship sacrificially to give God glory. You grow because you are living sacrificially. You serve sacrificially by being selfless. You give sacrificially, and it changes the way you live. You pray sacrificially because your prayers are ultimately about God, not you. You seek unity sacrificially by keeping the main thing the main thing.

Of all the seven basics of belonging, this one is the glue holding the others together. Healthy churches have healthy members who are willing to live sacrificially.

The Lifestyle of a Living Sacrifice

People are naturally drawn to extravagance. I doubt you hardly notice the 1998 Toyota Camry on the interstate. But if a Ferrari SF90 Stradale blew by you, I am sure it would garner your attention.

The television ratings for *Lifestyles of the Average and Ordinary* would probably not make the top-tier rankings. Most pastors do not make the celebrity list. Most churches do not make headlines.

The reason is our calling is not fame and fortune. Our calling is one of sacrifice. In reality, most of our churches are full of average people with normal lives. Church members, please don't miss God's grace in the normality of your routine. Normal days of emails, vacuuming, and PB&Js are amazing blessings. Pastors, don't let seeing the best and worst of people in their extremes cloud your judgment about who they really are.

Success in life is determined by faithfulness, not extravagance. Are you willing to exemplify the intentional paradox of being a living sacrifice? You are not ready to live unless you're willing to die. Jesus is our example. Jesus sacrificed His life for ours. He died on the cross for us. Jesus could have called on angels to spare Him, and it wouldn't have even been a battle. But He didn't. Jesus emptied Himself. He let go of the privileges of being God to save us. What did God give up for us? Everything. What are you going to give up for God?

Discussion Questions

1. Give an example of sacrifice. Why did you use this example?
2. How does sacrifice change the way you live?
3. What are some ways you can sacrifice for your church?
4. How should you put others before yourself?

CONCLUSION
I JOINED A CHURCH. NOW WHAT?

Congratulations! The choice to join a church is one that honors God, and I believe He will honor your commitment. Every church has a different way of assimilating new members. Make sure you follow the process given to you by church leadership.

Do you remember Jerry from the introduction?

He said, "The real reason you join a church is simple. Jesus is here."

There are many books on the church, and some of them are about church membership. I hope this book is helpful to you. But more than anything, I hope my writings prompt you to grow closer to Jesus through your local church.

The seven basics of belonging represent the foundation of church membership. As I mentioned previously, your church will have different doctrines, programs, schedules, and leadership than other churches. But every member should fulfill these seven basics of belonging in their local church.

1. Worship: Saying "yes" to God
2. Grow: Making disciples who make disciples
3. Serve: Reaching outward beyond yourself
4. Give: Honoring God with your offering
5. Pray: Prioritizing God's will through prayer
6. Seek unity: Keeping the main thing the main thing
7. Sacrifice: Putting others before yourself

Remember, church is like a family. Some families are healthier than others. Some churches are healthier than others. You will find a lot to like about your church. You will also find things you dislike. Make the decision now to be a helpful, not hurtful. Go ahead and commit to be part of the solution and not part of the problem. Even the healthiest churches will have sin issues because people are there. Adhering to the seven basics of belonging does not prevent problems, but they do keep you on the right track.

Kelly came up to her pastor after the worship

service with tears, "I've been here a little over a year, and I just need to tell you what this church means to me."

The pastor had no idea what she was about to say.

"You challenged me to start attending a small group, and I resisted. You insisted, so I went once for you. I've been every Sunday since that first visit."

She lifted her chin and took a deep breath.

"My brother recently got sick, and we didn't know if he would make it. My small group took the initiative and starting ministering to his family. They brought them meals and sent them cards. All I did was mention him in the prayer time. I asked them to pray once, and they ministered to him and his family for three months!"

"How is he?"

"Thankfully, better, but he still has a long way to go."

The Top Ten Next Steps for New Church Members

You joined a church. Now what? While every church has a different procedure of church membership, there are some simple things you can do to honor God in your decision. These items apply to everyone.

First, read your Bible every day. A national research study revealed something amazing. The number one way in which people grow spiritually is daily Bible reading, but only 35 percent of active churchgoers study their Bibles at least once a week. Ask anyone if they want to be healthier spiritually, and the likely answer is "yes." This study proves reading your Bible is the best path to spiritual maturity. The best next step you can make is to open your Bible every day and read God's Word.

Second, be active in weekly worship attendance. Another recent study showed that during the pandemic of 2020, the only group who improved in mental health were those who attended church weekly. While church attendance will not solve all your problems, the regular pattern and rhythm of being with the fellowship of the saints is good for your heart, mind, and soul.

Third, follow your church leadership. Most pastors and church leaders choose a life of sacrifice to serve others. They want to serve you! Blind loyalty is dangerous; only Jesus deserves unfettered commitment. But you should start with a posture of trust with your leadership.

Fourth, Encourage people around you. Encouragement is one of the most powerful and contagious forces in the church. The problem is discouragement is an even more powerful and contagious force. When you are an encourager, you can change the mood of just about everyone around you.

Fifth, invite others to church. One of my neighbors recently started attending our church. My wife invited her. Now my neighbor is inviting everyone else.

"I just love the church, and I'm telling people they will too!"

Believers have the responsibility to invite others into the body of Christ. But this responsibility is a joy. Seeing others light up as the find community is exciting and fulfilling.

Sixth, share Jesus with people in your life. Inviting other people to church shows you love the body of Christ. But you should also show your love of Jesus by sharing Him with others. I realize sharing your faith—often called evangelism—is a struggle for many believers. But it doesn't have to be. Live out your joy in Christ, and others will ask you about it. When they do, tell them about your salvation experience.

Seventh, join a group. Kelly is an excellent example. But her experience needs to be your experience. Your church will get bigger by getting smaller. People will stay in a church and grow in a church if they are part of a group. It is hard to connect personally with others in a worship gathering. When you are involved in a small group, you build relationships in a way that is not possible through the worship experience.

Eighth, pray every day for the ministries of your church and your church leaders. I have a few church members who remind me often about their daily prayers. One of the most encouraging things people say to me is, "I'm praying for you every day." I'll never forget one church member showing me his prayer journal. He made entries daily. My name was listed in every entry.

Ninth, start giving regularly. This commitment need not be controversial. If you believe in the mission of your church, then you should give to it.

Weekly or monthly giving is one of the best ways to invest in eternity. Frankly, you really don't give to your church. You are giving to God through your church. God does not need your money, but He does want your heart. Matthew's gospel makes it clear: "Wherever your treasure is, there the desires of your heart will also be." Where your money goes is where your heart goes.

Tenth, volunteer in a needed area of the church. Ask your church leaders about an area of need. Even if this area is not your preference or expertise, God will honor your desire to fill in a gap.

Church membership is an important part of following Christ. Enjoy the fellowship of believers at your church. Commit to God's mission with them. With your church, be an active agent of good in your community.

Allow me to offer a joyful "Welcome!" You belong here.

Discussion Questions

1. How can you get involved in your church?
2. What can you do to encourage church leaders?
3. How can you start supporting your church through giving?
4. Who can you invite to church?

APPENDIX
STUDY GUIDE FOR MEMBERSHIP CLASS

The following study guide accompanies the Church Answers resource: *The Complete Church Membership Class Toolkit*. The toolkit includes training sessions and online teaching sessions. Everything your church needs to facilitate a new members class.

You can find more about this resource at *churchanswers.com/completemembershipkit*. Use the code MEMBERS50 to receive 50% off at checkout.

STUDY GUIDE FOR MEMBERSHIP CLASS

Session 1

WHY JOIN A CHURCH?

The difference between attenders and members: _____!

Why would you join this church?

1. God's sovereignty
2. Your commitment
3. Community
4. Mission

Session 2

WORSHIP—SAYING "YES" TO GOD

A worshiping church desires God, not something from God.

_____ worship is using anything other than Jesus to get closer to God.

_____ worship is an awareness you are in the presence of God.

Key question: Are you willing to say "yes" to God? Are you willing to worship Him for who He is and not just what He provides?

Session 3

GROW—MAKING DISCIPLES WHO MAKE DISCIPLES

Whatever term you use, the Bible is clear: We are to grow.

1. Grow spiritually by becoming more mature in our faith
2. Grow numerically by multiplying ourselves by reaching others and pouring into others
3. The church is called to make disciples who make disciples

You need the church to grow spiritually because you can't grow _____.

Session 4

SERVE—REACHING OUTWARD BEYOND YOURSELF

Note: Doing church is like exercise. Once or twice a year, and it hurts. But a regular rhythm and pattern of worshiping, growing, and serving leads to spiritual health. Like physical exercise, spiritual health is not an instantaneous process but rather something that occurs over time.
An enduring church serves like Jesus.

Greatness in God's kingdom comes through _____.

Five steps to serving in your church.
1. Look for opportunities to serve in your church.
2. Volunteer where there is a need.
3. Take the initiative!
4. Invite your neighbors to church.
5. Share Jesus with people who will listen.

Session 5

GIVE—HONORING GOD WITH YOUR OFFERING

A _____ church gives to a _____ God.

Every _____ matters to God.
_____ giving changes you.

There are two types of greed:
1. Stuff: I want *more*.
2. Security: I want to be *safe*.

Session 6

PRAY—PRIORITIZING GOD'S WILL THROUGH PRAYER

Key question: Is prayer really that important?

The Bible is *not* about us. It's about God first. Proper prayer puts God first.

Your life should be an ongoing _____ with God.

How can you pray? P. R. A. Y.
    1. Praise
    2. Repent
    3. Ask
    4. Yield

Session 7

SEEK UNITY—KEEPING THE MAIN THING THE MAIN THING

A unified church is driven by love.

The healthiest churches inwardly are the most focused _____.

Unity *vs* Uniformity:
1. Unity: naturally occurs from within
2. Uniformity: typically forced from the outside

At the _____ of every healthy church is unity.

Session 8

SACRIFICE—PUTTING OTHERS BEFORE YOURSELF

Sacrifice means putting God's work above your _____.

Romans 12:1 and the paradox of a "living sacrifice." In many ways all the other basics of belonging lead up to this one.

1. You worship sacrificially to give God glory.
2. You grow because you are living sacrificially.
3. You serve sacrificially by being selfless.
4. You give sacrificially, and it changes the way you live.
5. You pray sacrificially because your prayers are ultimately about God, not you.
6. You seek unity sacrificially by keeping the main thing the main thing.

Healthy churches have healthy members who are willing to live sacrificially.

Session 9

I JOINED A CHURCH. NOW WHAT?

The top ten next steps for new church members.

1. Read your Bible every day.
2. Be active in weekly attendance.
3. Follow church leadership.
4. Encourage people around you, especially with unity.
5. Invite others to church.
6. Share Jesus with people in your life.
7. Join a group.
8. Pray every day for the ministries of your church and your church leaders.
9. Start giving regularly.
10. Volunteer in a needed area of the church.

THE COMPLETE MEMBERSHIP KIT

Everything your church needs
to facilitate a new members class.
The Complete Membership Kit includes:

- 4 training videos with Thom Rainer
- 9 teaching sessions for your congregation with Sam Rainer
- Lifetime access to training materials

Your new members will be able to articulate...

- **JOINING A CHURCH**
- **MAKING DISCIPLES**
- **OUTREACH**
- **CHURCH UNITY**
- **SACRIFICIAL GIVING**
- **AND MUCH MORE!**

Get 50% off the Total Membership Kit
when you use the coupon code at checkout

MEMBERS50

Go to:
www.churchanswers.com/completemembershipkit

Made in the USA
Middletown, DE
05 November 2023